The Sun

CHRISTINE TAYLOR-BUTLER

Children's Press®
An Imprint of Scholastic Inc.
New York Toronto London Auckland Sydney
Mexico City New Delhi Hong Kong
Danbury, Connecticut

Content Consultant

Bryan C. Dunne
Assistant Chair, Assistant Professor, Department of Astronomy
University of Illinois at Urbana–Champaign
Urbana, Illinois

Library of Congress Cataloging-in-Publication Data
Taylor-Butler, Christine, author.
The sun / by Christine Taylor-Butler.
    pages cm. — (A true book)
    Audience: Ages 9–12.
    Audience: Grades 4–6.
    ISBN 978-0-531-21157-1 (lib. bdg.) — ISBN 978-0-531-25363-2 (pbk.)
    1. Sun—Juvenile literature. I. Title. II. Series: True book.
    QB521.5.T425 2014
    523.7—dc23   2013027621

All rights reserved. Published in 2014 by Children's Press, an imprint of Scholastic Inc.
Printed in China 62
SCHOLASTIC, CHILDREN'S PRESS, A TRUE BOOK™, and associated logos are trademarks and/or registered trademarks of Scholastic Inc.

1 2 3 4 5 6 7 8 9 10 R 23 22 21 20 19 18 17 16 15 14

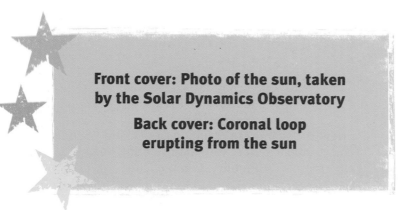

Front cover: Photo of the sun, taken by the Solar Dynamics Observatory

Back cover: Coronal loop erupting from the sun

Find the Truth!

Everything you are about to read is true *except* for one of the sentences on this page.

Which one is **TRUE**?

T or F The sun has enough fuel to burn forever.

T or F Solar flares can knock out power grids on Earth.

Find the answers in this book.

Contents

THE BIG TRUTH!

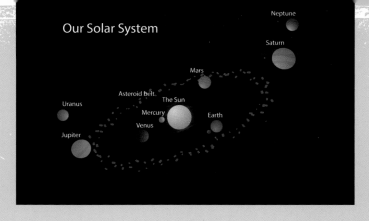

Our Solar System

Neptune
Saturn
Mars
Asteroid belt
The Sun
Uranus
Mercury
Venus
Earth
Jupiter

Our solar system includes eight planets orbiting the sun.

Spacecraft often have solar panels, allowing them to use the sun's energy for power.

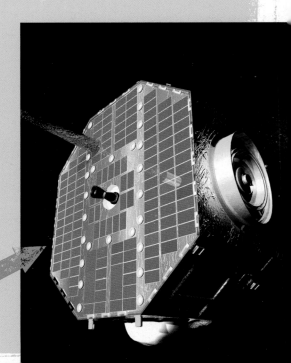

CHAPTER 1

The Star of the Solar System

Every day, the sun rises in the east and sets in the west. People set clocks based on its schedule. It provides warmth, light, and energy. The sun is such a normal part of life that people take it for granted. But without the sun, all life on Earth would end.

Don't look directly at the sun. Its bright light will damage your eyes.

A Giant Object

The sun is a star that sits in the center of our solar system. In fact, it drives the solar system. The sun's gravity keeps the **planets** and other objects orbiting around it. Scientists estimate that the sun is 4.6 billion years old. At some point, it will run out of fuel and die, but that will not happen in our lifetime. It still has at least 5 billion years of fuel left before it burns out.

Between the planets Mars and Jupiter, there is a ring of large rocky objects called asteroids.

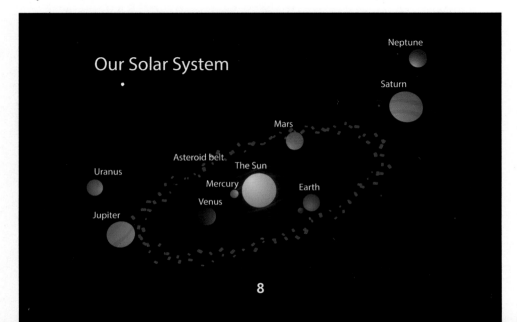

Our Solar System

Neptune

Saturn

Mars

Asteroid belt

Uranus

The Sun

Mercury

Earth

Venus

Jupiter

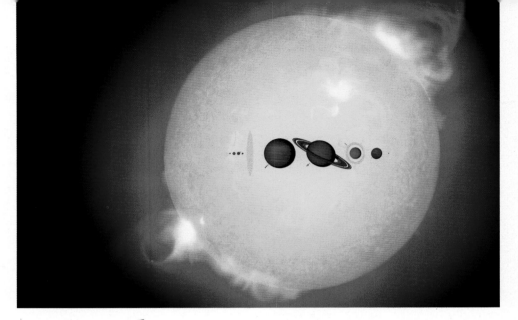

Even the solar system's largest planets are small compared to the sun.

The sun is halfway through its expected life span.

The sun is by far the largest object in our solar system. It contains 99.8 percent of the solar system's **mass**. The sun is so large that it could hold one million Earths inside it. If you measured around its **equator,** it would be 2.7 million miles (4.4 million kilometers). By comparison, Earth is only about 25,000 miles (40,000 km) around.

Earth is the third planet from the sun.

In Earth's sky, the sun does not look all that large. That is because the sun is so far away. Its average distance from Earth is 93 million miles (150 million km). Earth's orbit is not a perfect circle. Sometimes Earth is closer to the sun, and other times it is farther away. At its closest, Earth is about 91 million miles (147 million km) from the sun. At its farthest, Earth is 95 million miles (153 million km) away.

The Sun's Orbit

All the planets in our solar system orbit the sun. But does the sun have an orbit of its own? It does! The sun and our entire solar system orbit the center of our galaxy, the Milky Way. It takes about 230 million years to complete one trip together.

The solar system orbits the center of the Milky Way at 514,495 miles (828,000 km) per hour.

Sun

The Sun's Spin

Like Earth, the sun rotates on an axis. At the sun's equator, one rotation takes about 26 Earth days. Rotation at the north and south poles is slower. There it takes 35 Earth days to rotate. How can the sun's equator spin faster than its poles? The reason is that the sun is not solid. It is a giant ball of gases that all flow at different rates.

When the sun was younger, it rotated faster than it does today.

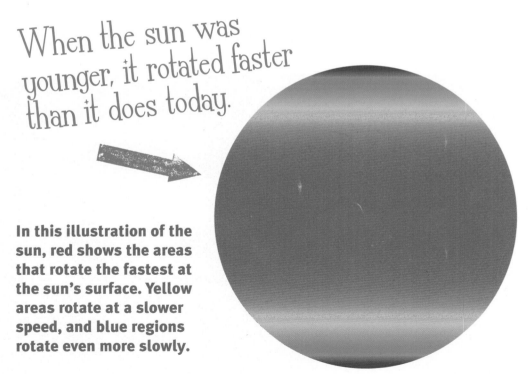

In this illustration of the sun, red shows the areas that rotate the fastest at the sun's surface. Yellow areas rotate at a slower speed, and blue regions rotate even more slowly.

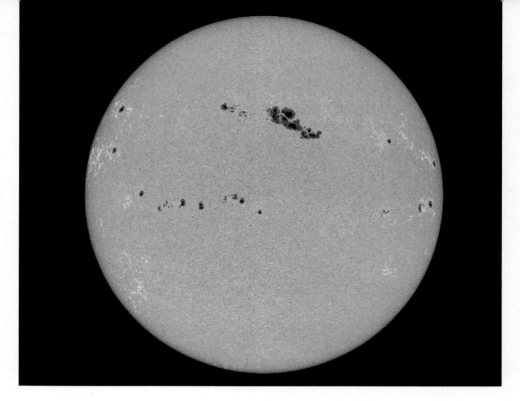

Sunspots appear as dark areas on the sun's surface.

Astronomers can calculate the speed of the sun's rotation by watching sunspots. These dark spots are patches that are cooler than the surrounding area. The fact that they are cooler makes them darker. Sunspots occasionally appear on the sun's surface. Scientists measure how quickly sunspots travel around the sun. This tells them how fast that part of the sun rotates.

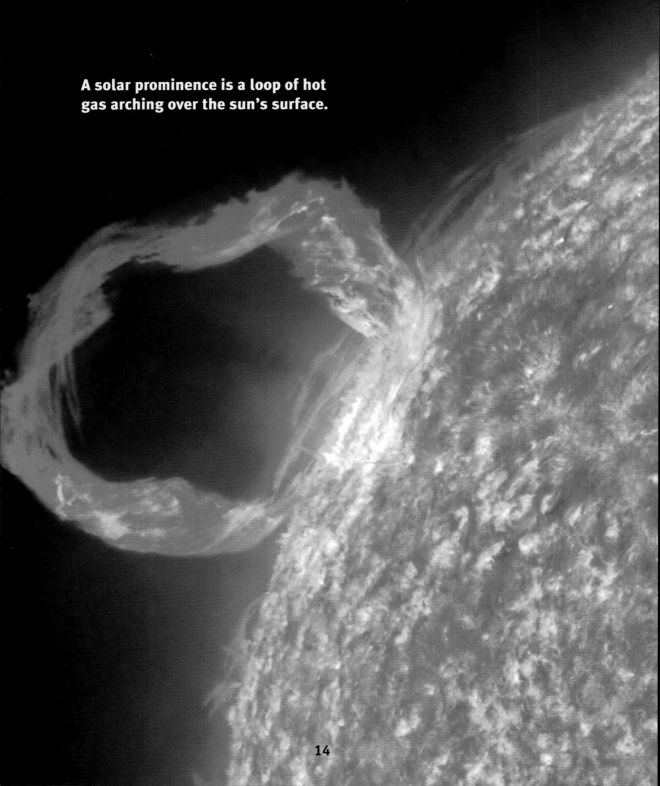

A solar prominence is a loop of hot gas arching over the sun's surface.

CHAPTER 2

The Sun's Energetic Layers

The sun is a giant **nuclear** engine. It is made up almost entirely of two chemical **elements**. About 90 percent of the sun is hydrogen. About 10 percent is helium. The sun also contains tiny traces of other elements, such as oxygen and carbon. Nuclear reactions in the core have powered the sun for billions of years. These reactions produce energy that travels up through the sun's layers to be released as light.

The average solar prominence is about 10 Earths across.

The Core

The sun's core is made of hot, **dense** gas. Temperatures reach 27 million degrees Fahrenheit (15 million degrees Celsius). In the intense heat, tightly packed hydrogen atoms smash against each other. The collision causes them to fuse together. This creates a new element: helium. Each second, 600 million tons of hydrogen are fused, becoming 596 million tons of helium. The remaining 4 million tons of matter become energy in the form of light.

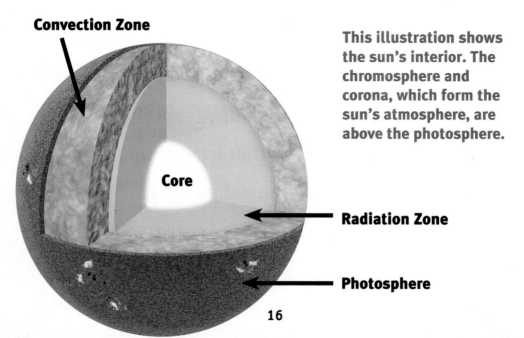

Convection Zone

Core

Radiation Zone

Photosphere

This illustration shows the sun's interior. The chromosphere and corona, which form the sun's atmosphere, are above the photosphere.

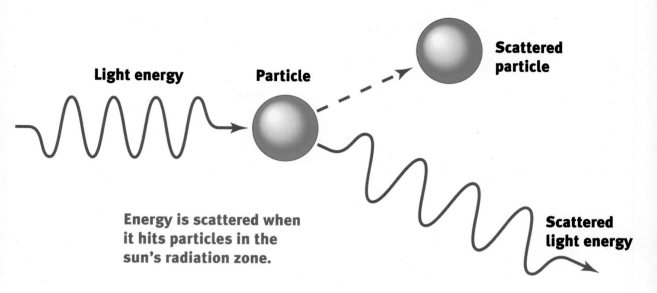

Light energy

Particle

Scattered particle

Energy is scattered when it hits particles in the sun's radiation zone.

Scattered light energy

The Radiation Zone

The light energy next passes through the sun's **radiation** zone. The light moves in a zigzag pattern, bouncing from atom to atom until it reaches the edge of the layer. Light is fast, traveling at roughly 186,000 miles (300,000 km) per second. But it bounces off a lot of atoms to make its way through the radiation zone. As a result, it takes about 170,000 Earth years to reach the next layer.

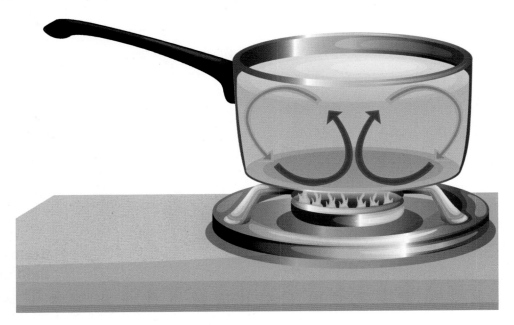

Convection in the sun is similar to convection in water as it boils in a pot. Hotter matter rises as cooler matter flows down.

Convection Zone

After passing through the sun's radiation zone, the light energy is carried through the next layer by **convection**. Hot gas rises and cooler gas sinks. The temperature falls between the sun's radiation and convection zones. The boundary area is a comparatively cool 3.6 million °F (2 million °C). It takes only a week for energy to move through the convection layer.

Photosphere

Above the convection zone is the sun's photosphere. This is the thin "surface" of the sun that we generally see. The temperature drops to 10,000°F (5,500°C) at the photosphere. The sun's light energy is released through the photosphere and travels to Earth.

It takes nearly 200,000 years for light to travel 435,000 miles (700,000 km) from the sun's core to the photosphere. But it takes only eight minutes to travel the 93 million miles (150 million km) to Earth!

Photosphere means "ball of light."

A lot of what we know about the sun comes from studying the photosphere. The photosphere's bumpy appearance is caused by rising bubbles and falling gases. The bubbles are called granules. The photosphere also features sunspots. Sunspots last for a few days to a few weeks and are highly magnetic. They often appear in pairs.

This close-up photo of the sun shows details of the granules that cover the photosphere.

Some astronomers refer to the chromosphere as the "dancing" layer.

Blasts of excess energy shoot through the chromosphere.

The Chromosphere

The chromosphere is above the photosphere. Think of the chromosphere as the sun's lower **atmosphere**. Temperatures rise in the chromosphere, reaching 45,000°F (25,000°C). In photographs, you may see fiery eruptions coming out of the sun. These are spicules and prominences. The flames shoot through the chromosphere and thousands of miles into space. Solar flares also shoot out of the chromosphere. These are sudden, bright flashes of magnetic energy.

The corona is too faint to be seen on a normal day. But during a solar eclipse, it becomes easy to spot.

The Corona

The outermost layer of the sun is the corona. It looks like a fiery halo around the sun. This layer is about 600,000 miles (1 million km) thick. The temperature here shoots up to 1.8 million °F (1 million °C). The corona produces the solar wind, a flow of energized particles that blast into space. The corona can be seen only during a solar eclipse. Eclipses occur when the moon blocks light from the sun's photosphere.

Auroras

What happens when the solar wind collides with our atmosphere? A light show called an **aurora**! The wind's particles transfer energy to oxygen and nitrogen in Earth's atmosphere. The energy is then released as light. Oxygen gives off green and red light. Nitrogen gives off purple and blue light. They sometimes mix and form other colors. Auroras are faint and can only be seen at night. They generally occur near Earth's polar regions.

The Solar Cycle

SEPT. 2010

Every 11 years, solar activity increases dramatically. This results in more sunspots, flares, prominences, and other activity. The sun's powerful magnetic field changes direction, too. The flip occurs when sunspot

MAY 2010

SEPT. 2012

SEPT. 2011

MARCH 2012

activity reaches its maximum level. The amount of activity then decreases before shooting back up in another 11 years. This is called the solar cycle.

Most sunspots start in a band that extends 35 degrees on either side of the equator. As solar activity increases, the sunspots move toward the equator. This forces the sun's north and south poles to switch.

The *Voyager 2* spacecraft is currently studying the edge of the heliosphere (blue), where it meets particles from the galaxy outside our solar system.

CHAPTER 3

Orbiting the Sun

The sun has many natural satellites. The best-known satellites are the planets: Mercury, Venus, Earth, Mars, Jupiter, Saturn, Uranus, and Neptune. There are also objects such as dwarf planets, comets, asteroids, and meteoroids. These objects all orbit the sun. The sun's **heliosphere** is like a giant magnetic bubble that encloses everything in the solar system.

 *Helios* comes from the Greek word for "sun."

The Perfect Place

Scientists nicknamed Earth "the Goldilocks planet." If it were closer to the sun, like Venus and Mercury, it would be scorching hot. If Earth were farther away, like Neptune and Uranus, it would be freezing cold. Instead, Earth is the perfect distance from the sun to support life. The sun helps our planet, but it also poses a danger.

Rainbows are caused when the sun's rays hit particles of water vapor in the atmosphere.

Earth's magnetic field (blue) helps protect the planet from the solar wind.

Solar Wind

Although the sun is millions of miles away, its energy reaches Earth quickly. For instance, the solar wind can travel at millions of miles per hour. Luckily, a layer of protection surrounds Earth. Our atmosphere and magnetic field block most of the dangerous, high-energy particles from reaching us.

Solar flares can affect signals from navigation satellites, making the satellites' information inaccurate.

Solar Flares

Solar flares are blasted from the sun when sunspots release magnetic energy. One blast is the same as 10 million volcanic eruptions. Coronal mass ejections (CMEs) occur in the corona. These sudden bursts of energy generate twice as much power as the amount of electricity generated in the entire United States. Solar flares and CMEs can disrupt Earth's power grids, communications systems, and navigation satellites.

Good for Us?

Humans must protect their skin and eyes from the sun's rays. But the sun provides benefits, too. It is a natural source of vitamin D. This nutrient is necessary for healthy hearts and cell growth. The sun's warmth makes life possible on Earth. Also, the sun is a renewable source of clean energy and light. The sun generates enough energy each second to power every home and business in the United States for 3.5 million years.

Sunscreen helps protect our skin from sunburn and other harmful effects of the sun.

31

Certain sects, or groups, in Hinduism celebrate the sun.

CHAPTER 4

Center of the Universe?

The sun is a constant influence on human life. We wake with it in the morning and fall asleep after it sets at night. Civilizations plan their harvests around its daily and seasonal positions in the sky. The sun's rays can even be harnessed as a source of energy. So it is not a surprise that the sun has been an important part of cultural and scientific ideas for thousands of years.

All planets, including Earth, orbit the sun in the same direction.

The Sun in Mythology

In ancient Egyptian mythology, the god of the sun was called Ra. Ra was reborn each morning, which humans saw as the sunrise. Aztecs believed the sun was a god in constant struggle with darkness. Chinese mythology described 10 suns that merged so they could appear in the sky at one time. This combination created tremendous heat. Inuit mythology tells of the sun goddess Malina, who is followed by her brother, Anningan the moon.

These ancient Egyptian drawings show worship of the god Ra.

Finding Center

People once believed
that the sun, moon,
planets, and stars orbited
Earth. Then, in the 16th
century, astronomer Nicolaus
Copernicus proposed that the
sun was the center of the universe. Government
leaders rejected his theory. In 1610, physicist
Galileo Galilei discovered moons orbiting Jupiter.
This showed that objects orbit bodies other than
Earth. He also saw Venus experience phases like
Earth's moon. These phases could be explained
only if Venus orbited the sun. Evidence like this
confirmed Copernicus's theories.

A Closer Look

Galileo first tracked sunspots through a telescope in the early 1600s. During that time, astronomer Christoph Scheiner created incredibly accurate drawings of sunspot locations. It was not until 1843 that anyone noticed sunspots occur in a cycle. Amateur astronomer Samuel Heinrich Schwabe made the first discovery. Astronomer Rudolf Wolf confirmed his findings soon after. Wolf also determined that the cycle lasts 11 years.

Timeline of Solar Study

1843

Samuel Heinrich Schwabe determines that sunspots experience a cycle.

Our Solar System

1610

Galileo discovers evidence that the sun is at the center of our solar system.

In 1833, astronomer John Herschel wrote that the sun's rays are the source of almost every motion on Earth. He suggested that the heat produces winds and helps grow vegetables. The vegetables then become the food for animals and people. The food provides energy, which animals and people need to live and grow. Herschel was right.

2008

The Interstellar Boundary Explorer begins to study solar wind particles reflected back from the edge of our solar system.

2010

The Solar Dynamics Observatory, the largest satellite to study the

Physicist Madhulika Guhathakurta helps lead efforts to understand the sun's effect on Earth. One satellite in the sun-focused STEREO program is pictured behind her.

38

CHAPTER 5

Solar Missions

The sun is a difficult target to study. Its energy is so immense it can overload instruments and fry electronics on any human-made satellite that comes close to it. Even small changes in the sun's activity can impact our planet. Now scientists are using new technology to get a closer look. They are also exploring the edges of the solar system to see how far the sun's influence extends.

 Scientists sometimes refer to solar activity as "space weather."

Solar Terrestrial Relations Observatory (STEREO)

STEREO launched in October 2006. It is actually two almost identical spacecraft that follow Earth's orbit. One orbits ahead of Earth, the other orbits behind. This allows the observatories to take photos of coronal mass ejections from two different angles. This creates a three-dimensional picture. The National Aeronautics and Space Administration (NASA) used the moon's gravity to help get STEREO into the right orbit.

The STEREO satellites follow the same orbit that Earth follows around the sun.

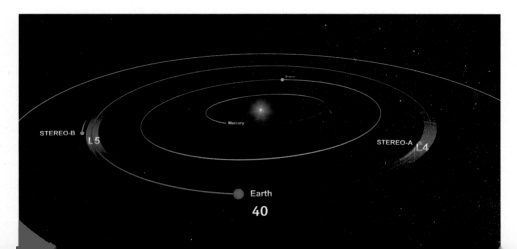

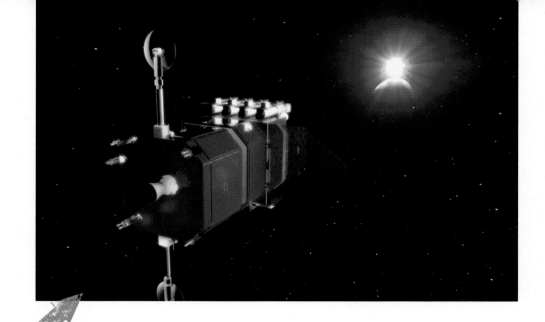

In three years, scientists collected almost 130 million images from SDO.

Solar Dynamics Observatory (SDO)

SDO is the largest solar exploration satellite ever built. It was launched in 2010 as part of NASA's Living with a Star Program. SDO's mission is to monitor changes in the sun's activity. The SDO satellite transmits up to 1.4 terabytes of data each day. Two radio antennas located in Las Cruces, New Mexico, capture this massive amount of data.

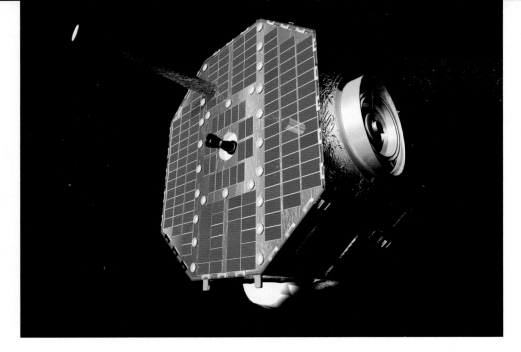

IBEX is about the size of a bus tire.

Interstellar Boundary Explorer (IBEX)

While most spacecraft analyze the sun directly, IBEX has another mission. It explores the outer boundary of the sun's magnetic field 10 billion miles (16 billion km) away. Launched in 2008, IBEX looks at where the solar wind meets particles from the Milky Way.

It is important to know about our sun. The more we learn, the better we can protect our planet from the sun's dangers and make use of the sun's benefits.

The End of a Star

Scientists say that billions of years from now, the sun will run out of fuel. Then it will expand into an enormous red giant. At this point, the sun will nearly reach Earth's orbit. The star's tremendous heat will boil away Earth's oceans and scorch the ground. Then the sun's outer gaseous layers will float away. A white dwarf will be left behind. This object will be about as wide as Earth, but with 200,000 times more mass. The white dwarf will slowly cool and fade, and eventually stop shining entirely.

True Statistics

Amount of matter converted into energy by the sun: 4 million tons per second

Speed of solar wind: 280 mi./sec. (450 km/sec)

Time it takes for energy to reach Earth's atmosphere: 8 minutes

Percent of the solar system's mass contained in the sun: 99.8

Speed of the fastest rotation on the sun's surface: 26 Earth days, at the equator

Speed of the slowest rotation on the sun's surface: 35 Earth days, at the poles

Hottest part of the sun: Core, at 27 million °F (15 million°C)

Coolest part on the sun: Photosphere, at 10,000°F (5,500°C)

Did you find the truth?

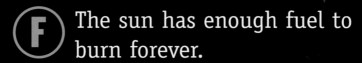

F The sun has enough fuel to burn forever.

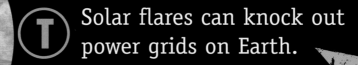

T Solar flares can knock out power grids on Earth.

Resources

Books

Aguilar, David A. *13 Planets: The Latest View of the Solar System.* Washington, DC: National Geographic, 2011.

Jemison, Mae, and Dana Meachen Rau. *Exploring Our Sun.* New York: Children's Press, 2013.

Jemison, Mae, and Dana Meachen Rau. *Journey Through Our Solar System.* New York: Children's Press, 2013.

Visit this Scholastic Web site for more information on the sun:
★ www.factsfornow.scholastic.com
Enter the keywords **The Sun**

Important Words

atmosphere (AT-muhs-feer) — the mixture of gases that surrounds a planet

aurora (uh-ROR-uh) — a colorful band of flashing lights that sometimes can be seen at night, especially near Earth's polar regions

convection (kuhn-VEK-shuhn) — the circulation of heat through liquids and gases

dense (DENS) — having a large amount of matter packed tightly together

elements (EL-uh-muhnts) —substances that cannot be divided up into simpler substances

equator (i-KWAY-tur) — an imaginary line around the middle of a planet or other body that is an equal distance from the north and south poles

heliosphere (HEE-lee-oh-sfeer) — the region of space encompassing our solar system that is influenced by the sun or solar wind

mass (MAS) — the amount of physical matter that an object contains

nuclear (NOO-klee-ur) — having to do with the energy created by splitting or fusing atoms

planets (PLAN-its) —large bodies orbiting a star

radiation (ray-dee-AY-shuhn) — energy given off in the form of light or heat

Index

Page numbers in **bold** indicate illustrations

About the Author

Christine Taylor-Butler is the author of more than 65 books for children including the True Book series on American History/Government, Health and the Human Body, and Science Experiments. A graduate of the Massachusetts Institute of Technology, Christine holds degrees in both civil engineering and art and design. She lives in Kansas City, Missouri.